CONTENTS

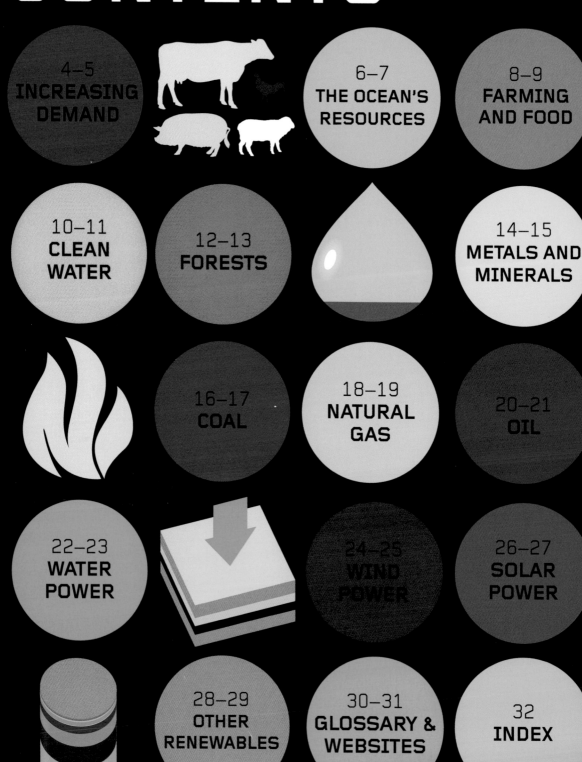

WELCOME TO THE WORLD OF INFOGRAPHICS

Using icons, graphics and pictograms, infographics visualise data and information in a whole new way!

DISCOVER HOW MUCH FOOD IS WASTED AROUND THE WORLD

SEE HOW MUCH WATER SUPPLIES ARE SHRINKING DUE TO HIGHER DEMAND

SEE WHICH COUNTRY IMPORTS THE MOST COAL

FIND OUT HOW MANY FARM ANIMALS ARE USED IN FOOD PRODUCTION AROUND THE WORLD

INCREASING DEMAND

Natural resources are naturally occuring substances that people can use to make objects, produce power or consume as food and drink. Many of these resources are limited, however, and their use is threatened by increasing demand.

A GROWING WORLD

At present, the world's population stands at more than 7 billion people. Over the next 60 years, improvements in health care and diet will see people living for longer and the world's population soar to more than 9 billion. This is more than twice the size it was 100 years before.

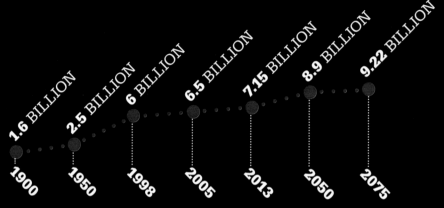

1.6 BILLION — 1900
2.5 BILLION — 1950
6 BILLION — 1998
6.5 BILLION — 2005
7.15 BILLION — 2013
8.9 BILLION — 2050
9.22 BILLION — 2075

Projected world population figures

2013
150,000

2015
190,000

2020
280,000

INCREASING DEMAND

Lithium is used to make batteries for hi-tech products, such as digital cameras. Increased demand for these will raise the need for this resource.

TANTALUM

Demand for this rare element that does not **corrode** has increased by 8–12 per cent each year since 1995, and **1,700 tonnes** is now produced each year.

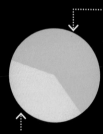

60% is used in the electronics industry

Nearly 1.3 billion people do not have electricity. It would cost

US$1 TRILLION

to meet full demand by 2030

MORE POWER

Increases in demand are not only due to an increase in the number of people. Better **living conditions** and improvements in supply will also increase demand. Up to 2035, rapid **industrialisation** in China and improvements in living conditions will see an increase in demand for electricity. Experts predict that demand for natural gas to fuel this increase will rise by more than

400%.

China's natural gas demand

How electricity is produced today

Oil and other liquids **1%**

Renewables **13%**

Nuclear **19%**

Natural gas **25%**

Coal **42%**

2011
130
BILLION CUBIC METRES

2035
545
BILLION CUBIC METRES

THE OCEAN'S RESOURCES

Seas and oceans cover more than two-thirds of the planet's surface. These waters provide millions of tonnes of food. Other sources include rivers, vast inland seas and enormous fish farms where sea creatures are reared.

FISHING NETS

Large commercial fishing boats use huge nets to catch fish. Many people believe that these large nets catch too many fish, destroying fish numbers and even damaging the sea floor. They also trap other sea creatures, including dolphins and turtles.

purse seine

midwater trawl

tangle net

bottom trawl

Lobster catching is a multi-billion-dollar industry, with nearly

200,000

tonnes caught each year.

That is the mass of more than

550 JUMBO JETS

OTHER OCEAN RESOURCES

The world's ocean waters hold nearly **20 million tonnes** of gold – each litre of seawater has, on average, 13 billionths of a gram dissolved in it.

That is enough for **2.83 kg** for every person on the planet.

HOW MUCH IS CAUGHT?

Every year, **131 million tonnes** of fish are caught and used for food – that is

18.8 kg
per person

the equivalent to **165 quarter-pounder burgers** for each person.

Where is it caught?

THE OCEANS' RICHEST FISHING GROUNDS

about **80 million tonnes** of fish are caught each year from seas and oceans

NW Pacific
20.9 million tonnes
(27%)

NE Atlantic
8.7 million tonnes
(11%)

West Central Pacific
11.7 million tonnes
(15%)

SE Pacific
7.8 million tonnes
(10%)

FISH FARMING

Asia has 87.3 per cent of the world's fishers and fish farmers, but only 68.7 per cent of the global production.

87.3%

68.7%

PRODUCTION RATES PER FISHER

 Asia **2.1 tonnes**

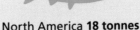 North America **18 tonnes**

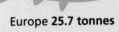 Europe **25.7 tonnes**

FARMING AND FOOD

Farming uses natural plant and animal resources to produce food, materials and even fuel. But even with today's improved techniques, can farmers produce enough to meet increased demand?

Percentage of the world's labour force

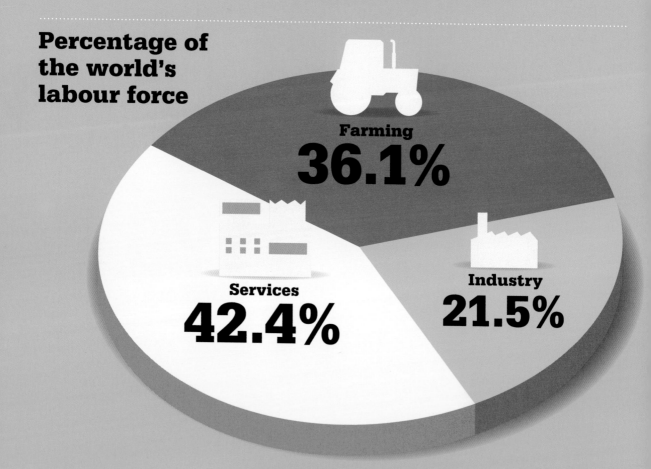

Farming
36.1%

Industry
21.5%

Services
42.4%

FARMERS AND FARM SIZE

European Union
13.7 million
farmers

average farm size
12 hectares

USA
2 million farmers

average farm size
180 hectares

IMPROVED PRODUCTION

In 1960, a single US farmer produced enough food to feed 26 people. Today, that has grown to 155 people. This is due to improvements in farming technology and techniques.

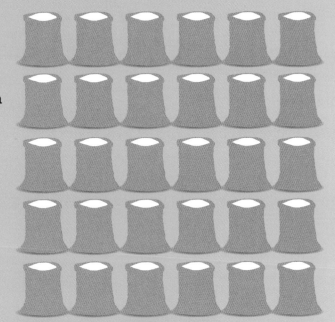

1960

TODAY

Waste

More than **30 per cent** of all food produced on the planet is wasted. That comes to about

1.2-2
BILLION TONNES.

30%

2 billion people could be fed with the amount of food the USA alone throws away each year.

FARM ANIMALS

At present, people around the world use

60,000,000,000

farm animals each year for milk, meat and eggs.

This is set to rise to

120,000,000,000

by 2050.

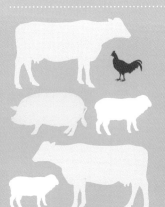

TODAY
(nearly nine for every person)

2050
(nearly 14 for every person)

CLEAN WATER

Water is vital for every living thing – without it, life would not be possible. However, while some people have plenty of water, many others struggle to get enough to survive.

PROBLEMS WITH ACCESS TO CLEAN WATER

Around the world,

780,000,000

people lack access to clean water...

... more than **2.5 times** the population of the USA.

Rest of the world
433 million

Of these, **343 million** live in Africa,

while just **4 million** live in the Europe AND North America.

2,190 KM

In Africa and Asia, people walk an average distance of nearly 6 km each day to collect water. In a year, the average distance walked is 2,190 km.

Who uses the most?

=2 litres

Americans use **380 LITRES** of water per day

People living in sub-Saharan Africa use **19 LITRES**

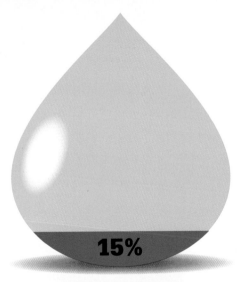

15%

HOW WATER IS USED

Livestock production demands 15 per cent of all the world's irrigation water.

DECLINING STOCKS

Underground aquifers are a key source of clean water.

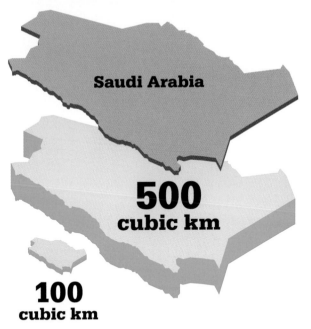

Saudi Arabia

500 cubic km

100 cubic km

When intensive farming started **40 years ago**, there was an estimated **500 cubic km** of water beneath Saudi Arabia. With demand from farming and very little rain, that has now been reduced by **80 per cent** to an estimated **100 cubic km**.

Each year, India uses **70 cubic km** more groundwater than is replaced by rain. Other countries who are using more groundwater than is replenished are:

Pakistan		35 cubic km
USA		30 cubic km
China		30 cubic km

Globally, the rate of over-use of groundwater is

250 cubic km

Around the world, an estimated **200 million hours** are spent each day **collecting water.**

that is more than 1.5 times Lake Tahoe, USA.

FORESTS

The world's forests are a key source of many resources, including fuel and building materials. They are also home to many valuable plants and animals that can be used for food and medicines.

SIZE OF FOREST RESOURCES

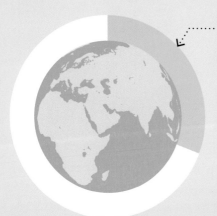

Forests cover **31%** of the world's land area:

4 billion hectares (40 million sq km)

about **6,000 sq metres** for every person

just bigger than the size of a football pitch.

Together, five countries (Russia, Brazil, Canada, USA and China) have more than half of the world's total forest area.

WHAT DO FORESTS PRODUCE?

Global trade in non-wood forest products, such as bamboo, mushrooms, game, fruit, medicinal plants, fibre, gum and resins, is estimated at

US$11,000,000,000

23% of the world's population depend on forests for fuel, food, grazing areas and medicine.

23%

More than 25 per cent of modern medicines originate from tropical forest plants, with an annual value of

US$108 billion.

25%

FORESTS UNDER THREAT

Fires, the expansion of farmland and changes in climate conditions have all been causes in the reduction of the amount of forest land around the world.

Between **1990 and 2000**, the rate of deforestation was

83,000 sq km
per year.

equivalent to an area of **Austria** every year.

Between **2000 and 2010**, the annual rate of deforestation was

52,000 sq km.

equivalent to the area of **Costa Rica**

This is a decline in the rate of deforestation of nearly

40%

WHO PRODUCES THE MOST FOREST PRODUCTS?

Paper and paperboard

China **26%**

USA **19%**

Germany **6%**

Japan **7%**

Canada **3%**

Rest of the world **39%**

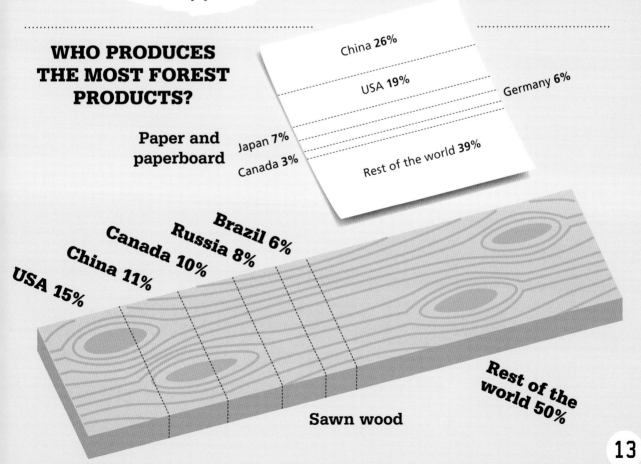

USA **15%**

China **11%**

Canada **10%**

Russia **8%**

Brazil **6%**

Rest of the world **50%**

Sawn wood

METALS AND MINERALS

Many resources, including minerals and metals, lie buried deep beneath the ground. Getting them to the surface involves some of the biggest machines and vehicles ever built.

HOW ARE MINERALS MINED?

Different mining techniques are used depending on where the resources are buried and the type of rock above them.

MOUNTAIN TOP
The entire top of a hill or mountain is removed to reach the minerals beneath.

CONTOUR
The rock lying above the minerals and running around the contours of a hill is removed.

OPEN-PIT AND STRIP MINES
A large area of rock is stripped clear to reach the minerals buried beneath.

DRIFT MINE
A horizontal tunnel is cut directly into the rock to reach minerals.

There are **60** different **minerals** found in a single **computer chip**, including **silicon, copper, gold** and **tin.**

How minerals are combined and altered

How iron ore is turned into steel

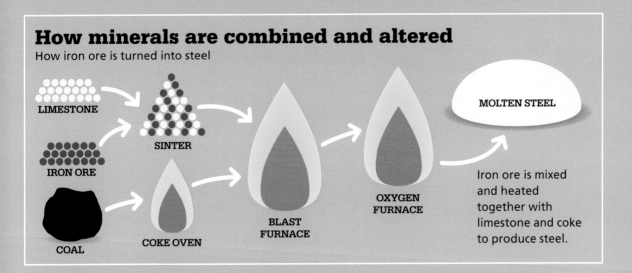

LIMESTONE

SINTER

IRON ORE

COAL

COKE OVEN

BLAST FURNACE

OXYGEN FURNACE

MOLTEN STEEL

Iron ore is mixed and heated together with limestone and coke to produce steel.

PRODUCTION LEVELS AND USES

Copper 17 million tonnes ——— Used in cables, pipes, roofing

Gold 2,700 tonnes • Used in jewellery, dentistry, medicine

Lead 5.2 million tonnes ——— Used in roofing

Platinum 179 tonnes • Used in jewellery, electrical equipment

Zinc 13 million tonnes ———

Used in galvanising and protecting metals, coins

World mineral production

URANIUM

Uranium is used in nuclear reactors to produce electricity.

1 TONNE URANIUM

=

16,000 TONNES OF COAL

=

80,000 BARRELS OF OIL.

=

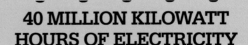

40 MILLION KILOWATT HOURS OF ELECTRICITY

SLOPE MINE
A sloping tunnel leads down to minerals buried underground.

SHAFT MINE
Long shafts are dug straight down to reach minerals far underground.

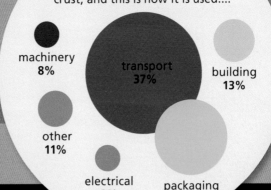

Aluminium
is one of the most abundant metal elements in the Earth's crust, and this is how it is used....

machinery 8%

transport 37%

building 13%

other 11%

electrical 8%

packaging 23%

COAL

This fossil fuel is formed from the remains of plants that died millions of years ago. It is burned in homes for heat, or in power stations to produce electricity.

How coal is formed

Over millions of years, dead plants are covered by layers of soil and form coal.

2. As more soil layers formed, the weight squeezed together the remains of the buried plants.

1. Millions of years ago, rotting plants from forests were gradually covered up by soil.

3. Heat from the inside of the Earth and the weight of the upper layers transformed the remains into coal.

Who produces the most?

(million tonnes)

USA 1,004

INDIA 586

CHINA 3,576

AUSTRALIA 414

INDONESIA 376

Who imports the most?

(tonnes)

CHINA 190,000,000

JAPAN 175,000,000

GERMANY 41,000,000

CHINESE TAIPEI 66,000,000

HOW MUCH COAL IS LEFT?

It is estimated that there are more than **3 trillion tonnes** of coal left in the USA...

... only about **235 billion tonnes** of this can be mined using present-day technology.

If coal production grows at its present rate, this will be exhausted in less than 170 years.

20%
of global greenhouse gas emissions

Side effects of using coal
While burning coal produces energy for heating and generates electricity, it also releases greenhouse gases. These are thought to be a major cause of global warming.

WHO HAS THE MOST COAL?
(world coal reserves)

Russia 18.3%

USA 27.5%

Europe and Eurasia 17.2%

China 13.3%

Africa 3.7%

India 7.0%

Central and South America 0.9%

Australia and NZ 8.9%

● Rest of the World 3.2%

SOUTH KOREA 129,000,000

UK 33,000,000

INDIA 105,000,000

NATURAL GAS

Like coal, natural gas is a fossil fuel that is burned in power stations to produce electricity. This non-renewable fuel is also piped into homes, where it is used for heating and cooking.

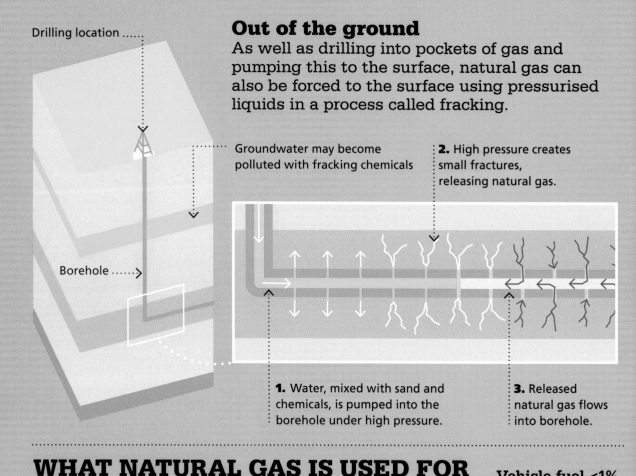

Out of the ground

As well as drilling into pockets of gas and pumping this to the surface, natural gas can also be forced to the surface using pressurised liquids in a process called fracking.

Drilling location ......

Borehole ......>

Groundwater may become polluted with fracking chemicals

2. High pressure creates small fractures, releasing natural gas.

1. Water, mixed with sand and chemicals, is pumped into the borehole under high pressure.

3. Released natural gas flows into borehole.

WHAT NATURAL GAS IS USED FOR

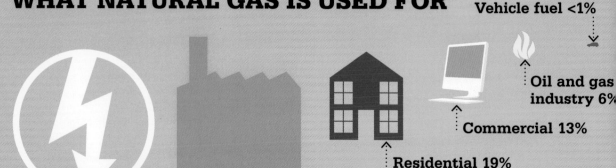

Vehicle fuel <1%

Oil and gas industry 6%

Commercial 13%

Residential 19%

Industrial 28%

Electric power 31%

Pipeline and distribution <3% ····>●

Who produces the most
(billion cubic metres)

RUSSIA
677

USA
651

CANADA
160

QATAR
151

IRAN
149

NATURAL GAS FACTS

Natural gas is odourless and colourless. Gas companies add a substance called mercaptan, which smells like rotten eggs, so that gas leaks are noticeable.

To transport it, natural gas is chilled to about -160°C, when it turns into a liquid.

It becomes 600 times smaller. This is the same as shrinking a football down to a marble with a diameter of about 2.6 cm.

0°C: Melting point of water

-89.2°C Lowest recorded temperature on Earth (Vostok Station, Antarctica)

-160°C

USA
683.3

EU
515

IRAN
137.5

CHINA
129

RUSSIA
414.1

Who uses the most
(billion cubic metres)

OIL

Crude oil is usually formed from the bodies of tiny dead organisms, such as plankton and algae. These were buried millions of years ago. Pressure and high temperature then turned them into oil.

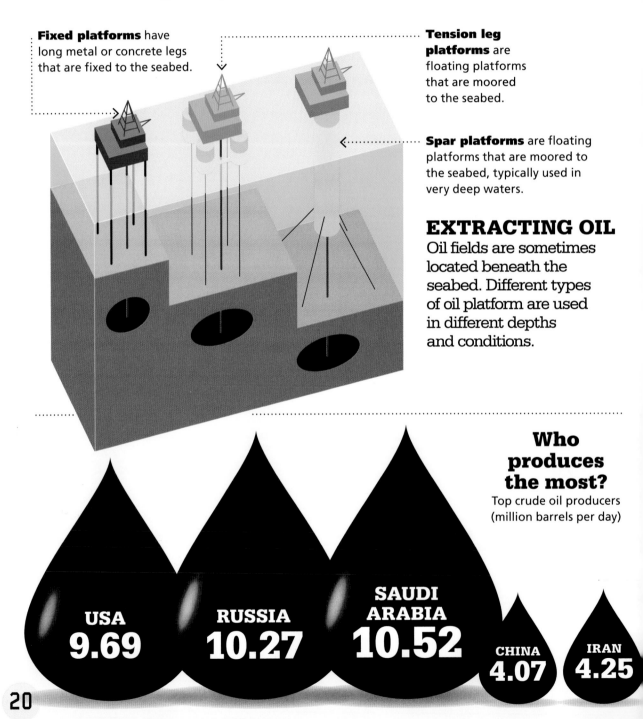

Fixed platforms have long metal or concrete legs that are fixed to the seabed.

Tension leg platforms are floating platforms that are moored to the seabed.

Spar platforms are floating platforms that are moored to the seabed, typically used in very deep waters.

EXTRACTING OIL

Oil fields are sometimes located beneath the seabed. Different types of oil platform are used in different depths and conditions.

Who produces the most?

Top crude oil producers (million barrels per day)

USA
9.69

RUSSIA
10.27

SAUDI ARABIA
10.52

CHINA
4.07

IRAN
4.25

WHAT CRUDE OIL IS TURNED INTO

A **159 litre** barrel of crude oil makes about
170 litres of petroleum products:

Heavy fuel oil **3.8 litres**

Other distillates (heating oil) **3.8 litres**

Liquid Petroleum Gas (LPG) **7.6 litres**

Jet fuel **15.1 litres**

Other products **26.3 litres**
Diesel **41.5 litres**

Petrol **71.9 litres**

OTHER PRODUCTS INCLUDE ink, crayons, dishwashing liquids, deodorant, eyeglasses, CDs and DVDs, tyres, ammonia and heart valves.

HOW MUCH IS USED?

Every day, Americans use on average about

136 billion litres of petrol.

The USA uses **18.9 million** barrels of crude oil every day.

Top exporters
(million barrels per day)

RUSSIA
7.1

UAE
2.4

IRAN
2.5

NIGERIA
2.3

SAUDI ARABIA
8.5

21

WATER POWER

Renewable resources are those that can be used over and over again. Flowing water in rivers and the sea has been used as a power source for thousands of years.

HOW MUCH POWER IS PRODUCED

Hydroelectric power provides **20 per cent** of the entire world's electricity.

Other sources **80%**

Hydroelectric

World's biggest producers
(percentage of world total)

CHINA 19.8

BRAZIL 12.3

CANADA 10.8

Between them, the USA, China, Canada and Brazil produced more than **50 per cent** of the world's hydroelectric electricity.

USA 9.4

THREE GORGES DAM

Three Gorges Dam **186 M**

Washington monument **169 M**

Taller than the Washington monument and **2 KM WIDE**

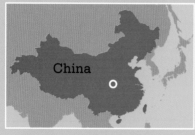
China

The Three Gorges Dam in China is one of the biggest hydroelectric power stations in the world.

Weight of the water (estimated at more than 300 million tonnes) may cause earthquakes in the area.

cost to build:

US$37 BILLION

Generates 11 times as much electricity as the Hoover Dam, USA.

Relocated 1.3 million people (13 cities, 140 towns, and 1,350 villages)

HYDROELECTRIC DAM

A dam creates a large lake from which water can be channelled past bladed wheels called turbines, sending them spinning. The turbines are connected to generators, which produce electricity.

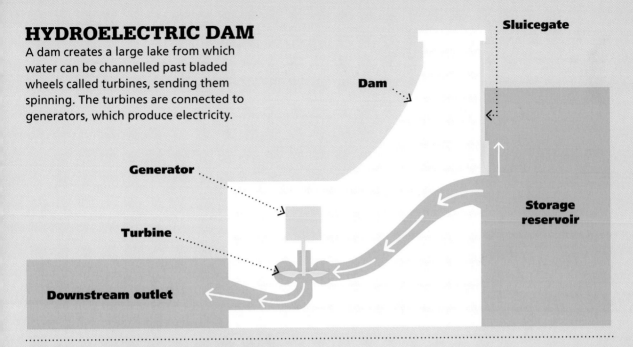

Sluicegate

Dam

Generator

Turbine

Downstream outlet

Storage reservoir

TIDAL POWER STATIONS

Every day, the world's seas and oceans rise and fall with the tides. This movement can be harnessed to produce electricity.

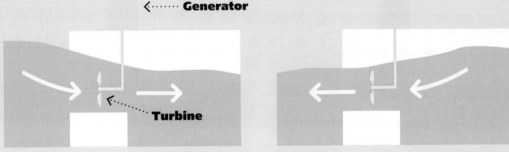

Generator

Turbine

1. As the tide comes in, the flowing water spins turbines. The turbines are connected to generators to produce electricity.

2. The same thing happens when the tide goes out. The water may flow the other way, but the turbine still spins and the generator still produces electricity.

HOW WAVE POWER WORKS

This generator uses the movement of waves to produce electricity. Experimental and working wave generators can be found off the coasts of the USA, UK, Australia and Sweden.

Jointed parts rock up and down as the waves move past. This movement is used to generate power.

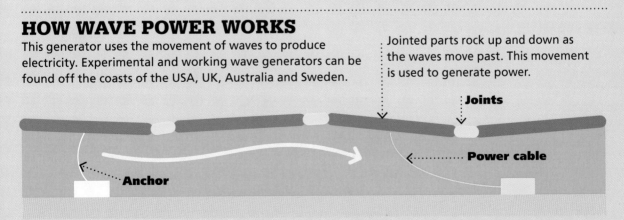

Joints

Power cable

Anchor

WIND POWER

Early windmills used the power of the wind to pump water and grind crops to make flour. Today, huge wind farms with thousands of turbines produce power for millions of people.

HOW MODERN WIND TURBINES WORK

Wind turbines catch the wind using tall, propeller-like blades. These are connected to a generator, which produces electricity as the blades spin.

Turbine blade

Main shaft spins around with the blades.

Gearbox transfers spinning movement to the generator.

Generator produces electricity as the blades spin around.

GRINDING CROPS

Traditional windmills used large sails to catch the wind, sending them spinning. This movement was transferred to huge millstones, which ground crops between them to produce flour.

Windmill sails

Cogs and shafts turned by the wind

Flour

Millstones

Tower holds the blades high. The turbine can rotate so that the blades face into the wind.

How much power is produced using the wind?
(megawatts)

INDIA 18,421

SPAIN 22,796

GERMANY 31,332

USA 60,007

CHINA 75,564

Denmark generates nearly **20 per cent** of its electricity supply using more than **5,000** wind turbines – nearly one turbine for every **1,000** Danish people.

TURBINE TYPES

There are two main types of wind turbine. Horizontal axis turbines have the main shaft arranged horizontally, while vertical axis turbines have their shafts arranged vertically.

The world's largest windfarm,

the Horse Hollow Wind Energy Center in Texas, USA, has

421

wind turbines and generates enough electricity to power

220,000

homes per year.

Vertical axis

Horizontal axis

SOLAR POWER

Every hour, the Sun beams more than enough energy at the Earth to meet global demand for a whole year. However, the amount that can be used to produce electricity depends on where you live.

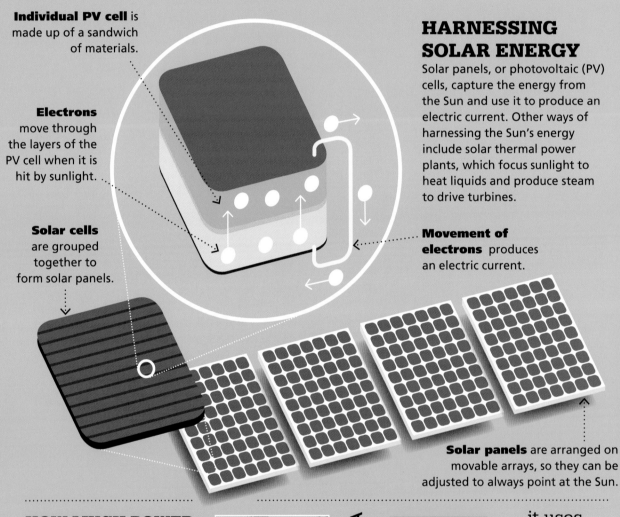

Individual PV cell is made up of a sandwich of materials.

Electrons move through the layers of the PV cell when it is hit by sunlight.

Solar cells are grouped together to form solar panels.

HARNESSING SOLAR ENERGY

Solar panels, or photovoltaic (PV) cells, capture the energy from the Sun and use it to produce an electric current. Other ways of harnessing the Sun's energy include solar thermal power plants, which focus sunlight to heat liquids and produce steam to drive turbines.

Movement of electrons produces an electric current.

Solar panels are arranged on movable arrays, so they can be adjusted to always point at the Sun.

HOW MUCH POWER CAN BE PRODUCED?

One of the world's largest solar thermal power plants is in Andalusia, Spain.

Spain

COVERS AN AREA EQUIVALENT TO

210 football pitches

it uses **600,000** mirrors

it generates **150 megawatts** of electricity – enough for a city of **500,000**

One of the biggest solar PV power stations in the world in Gujarat, India, produces

600 MEGAWATTS

enough to supply the power for nearly **400,000** homes in the USA.

On a sunny day at noon, each square metre of the Earth's surface receives around

1 kilowatt

of solar power – the equivalent power used by a fridge.

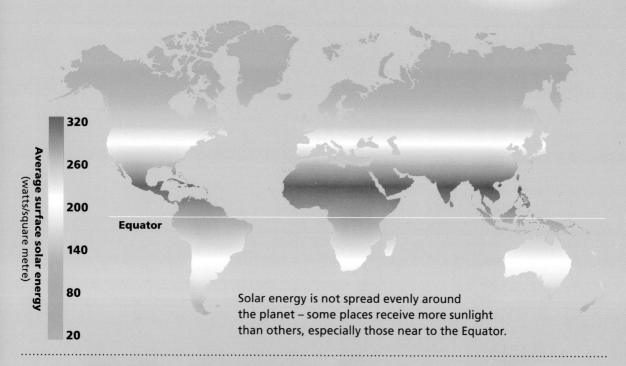

Average surface solar energy (watts/square metre)

320
260
200
140
80
20

Equator

Solar energy is not spread evenly around the planet – some places receive more sunlight than others, especially those near to the Equator.

88.738 km/h

Solar cells

The record speed for a solar powered car is 88.738 km/h set by Sunswift IV in Australia on 7 January 2011.

OTHER RENEWABLES

Renewable sources of energy also include plant and animal products, as well as harnessing the enormous amounts of heat produced at the Earth's core.

GEOTHERMAL ENERGY

Temperatures beneath the Earth's surface increase as you get closer to the planet's core. Things become so hot, that rock melts and flows as a superhot runny liquid. By drilling down through the Earth's crust, this energy can be used to heat water, producing steam to power turbines and produce electricity.

Core
4,900–
6,100°C

Outer core
4,500–
5,500°C

Surface
15°C

0°C

Surface

Outer core

Core

Cross-section of the Earth

4. Steam is used to spin turbines, which are connected to generators to produce electricity.

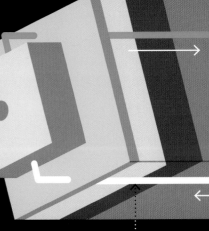

Geothermal power plants are built in areas where the Earth's heat rises close to the surface

HOW CLEAN IS GEOTHERMAL ENERGY?

Geothermal power plants produce less than 1 per cent of the carbon dioxide emissions of a fossil fuel plant...

97%

1%

...and emit 97 per cent fewer sulphur compounds than fossil fuel plants. Sulphur compounds are the cause of acid rain.

Geothermal plants can cause problems. These include the release of hydrogen sulphide (smells like rotten eggs) and some geothermal fluids, which may contain toxic substances.

1. Water is pumped down through boreholes.

2. Hot rocks heat the water, producing steam.

3. Steam rises back to the surface through boreholes.

Biggest producers of wood fuel

India 16%

China 10%

Brazil 8%

Ethiopia 5%

Biofuels

Most of the energy on our planet comes from the Sun. Plants use this solar energy to produce food for themselves and for other living things to eat. These energy stores can be used and converted into biofuels, such as wood, methane and ethanol.

Sun

Plants

Animals

Methane (gas)

Wood (solid)

Sugar

Ethanol (liquid)

Chlorophyll

Photosynthesis

Chlorophyll is found inside many plant cells. It plays an important part in photosynthesis, where the Sun's energy is used to produce sugars. The sugars in some crops, including corn and sugar cane, can be refined to produce biofuels, such as ethanol.

GLOSSARY

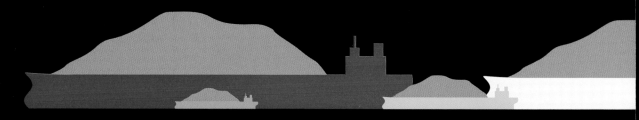

acid rain
Rain that contains high levels of man-made pollutants. It is caused by burning fuels in factories, power stations, cars and elsewhere, and can damage buildings and the natural environment.

aquifer
An underground layer of rock that contains a lot of water, which can be used to supply wells.

biofuel
Fuel derived from renewable natural resources, such as crops.

blast furnace
A very hot oven for making iron in which the temperature is raised by blasts of air.

borehole
A tunnel drilled into the ground and often used to look for, or access, natural resources.

deforestation
The cutting down of large areas of forest.

coke oven
An oven for converting coal, a fuel with many impurities, into coke, a much purer fuel.

crude oil
Oil in its natural state before it is converted, or refined, into useful products, such as petrol.

element
A substance that cannot be broken down into any other substances.

fossil fuel
A fuel made from the decayed remains of dead organisms. Coal and oil and are fossil fuels.

galvanising
Covering iron or steel with a rust-resistant coating of zinc.

geothermal energy
Energy derived from the heat of the Earth's interior.

global warming
A gradual increase in the Earth's average temperature.

greenhouse gases
Gases, such as carbon dioxide and methane, which can trap heat in the atmosphere. This effect is similar to how the glass in a greenhouse traps the Sun's heat.

groundwater
Water that lies beneath the Earth's surface.

oxygen furnace
A very hot oven in which pure oxygen is blown through molten iron to make steel.

hydroelectric power
Electricity made by harnessing the power of flowing water.

industrialisation
The rapid development of industries.

mineral
A naturally occuring substance made of one – or usually several – elements.

non-renewable
Something that can be used only once. Coal is a non-renewable fuel source.

ore
A type of mineral that contains metals.

renewable
Something that can be replaced after it has been used. Wind and wave power are renewable energy sources.

refined
Processed to remove the impurities and create new products. For instance, oil is refined to produce petrol.

sinter
A mixture of iron ore and limestone used in the production of steel.

watt
A unit of energy; 1,000 watts equals a kilowatt, while 1,000 kilowatts equals a megawatt.

Websites

MORE INFO:
http://www.nrdc.org/reference/kids.asp
The kids' section of the Natural Resources Defense Council provides links to sites dedicated to natural resources and environmental protection.

www.sciencenewsforkids.org
Information on the latest technological breakthroughs, and lots of games and facts about the world of science and resources.

www.sciencemuseum.org.uk/onlinestuff.aspx
Online science games and activities from the UK's Science Museum, plus plenty of other resources for kids.

MORE GRAPHICS:
www.visualinformation.info
A website that contains a whole host of infographic material on subjects as diverse as natural history, science, sport and computer games.

www.coolinfographics.com
A collection of infographics and data visualisations from other online resources, magazines and newspapers.

www.dailyinfographic.com
A comprehensive collection of infographics on an enormous range of topics that is updated every single day!

INDEX

ACKNOWLEDGEMENTS

Published in paperback in 2014 by Wayland
Copyright © Wayland 2014

Wayland
338 Euston Road
London NW1 3BH

Wayland Australia
Level 17/207 Kent Street
Sydney NSW 2000

All rights reserved.
Senior editor: Julia Adams

Produced by Tall Tree Ltd
Editors: Jon Richards and Joe Fullman
Designer: Ed Simkins
Consultant: Kim Bryan

Dewey classification: 333.7

ISBN: 9780750283205

10 9 8 7 6 5 4 3 2 1

Printed in Malaysia

Wayland is a division of Hachette
Children's Books, an Hachette UK company.
www.hachette.co.uk

The website addresses (URLs) included in this book were valid at the time of going to press. However, because of the nature of the Internet, it is possible that some addresses may have changed, or sites may have changed or closed down, since publication. While the author and Publisher regret any inconvenience this may cause the readers, no responsibility for any such changes can be accepted by either the author or the Publisher.